STEP-BY-STEP
Addition and
Subtraction

LINWORTH
LEARNING

From the Minds of Teachers

Linworth Publishing, Inc.
Worthington, Ohio

Cataloging-in-Publication Data

Editor: Claire Morris

Design and Production: Good Neighbor Press, Inc.

Published by Linworth Publishing, Inc.
480 East Wilson Bridge Road, Suite L
Worthington, Ohio 43085

ISBN: 1-58683-141-0

5 4 3 2 1

Table of Contents

Introduction

The goal of this book is mastery of single-digit addition and subtraction for the Pre-K–2 student. Computational fluency is achieved through meaningful, step-by-step, practice exercises emphasizing number recognition and addition and subtraction facts through 12. Central to the structure of the book is the knowledge that the foundation of early mathematical understanding is counting. Children love to count, and this book builds on their natural propensity to solve everyday mathematical operations through the counting of concrete objects. The pairing of numbers with picture equivalents for every operation in this book reinforces and facilitates children's ability to think about and remember numbers in the absence of physical models. The material in Step-by-Step Addition and Subtraction correlates with the national curriculum standards for numbers and operations for the Pre-K–2 student set by the National Council of Teachers of Math. An answer key is provided at the back of the book.

Recognizing Numbers One to Five

Directions: Count the balloons. Write the number in the box.

Recognizing Numbers Five to Ten

Directions: Count the number of pictures in each rectangle. Write the number on the line.

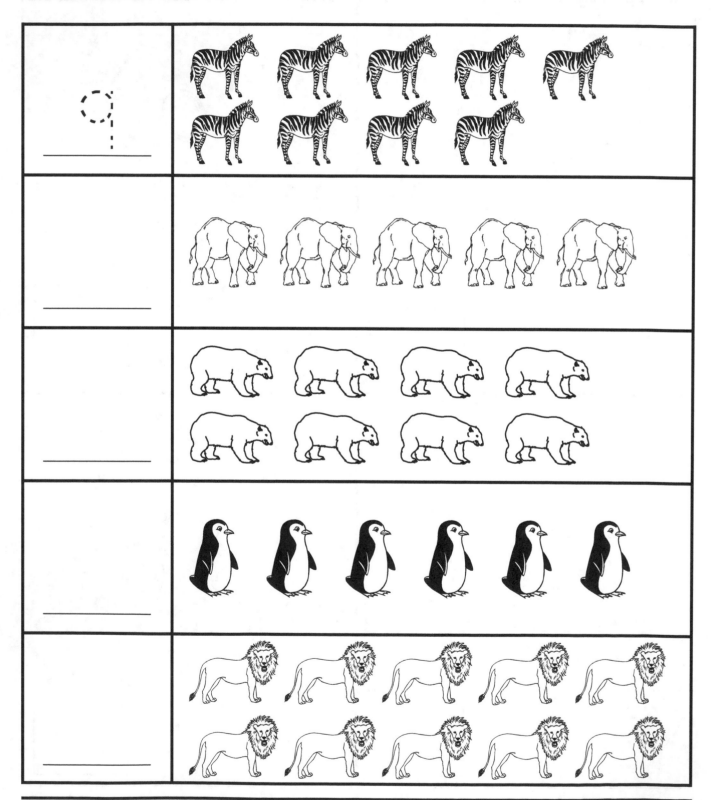

_____

_____

_____

_____

_____

Recognizing Numbers Ten to Twelve

Directions: Count the pictures. Write the number in the box.

10

 # Addition

Directions: Add the pictures. Write the answer on the line.

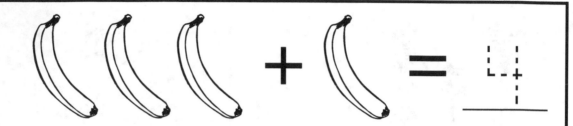 = 4

 = _____

 = _____

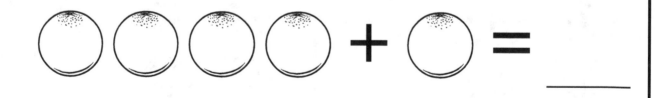 = _____

 = _____

 = _____

 Addition

Directions: Add the pictures. Write the answer on the line.

📕 📕 📕 **+** 📘 📘 📘 📘 **=** 7
_____

📏 📏 **+** 📏 📏 📏 **=**
_____

🌐 🌐 🌐 🌐 🌐 **+** 🌐 🌐 🌐 **=**
_____

✂✂✂ ✂✂✂ **+** ✂✂ ✂✂✂ **=**
_____

🖍 🖍 🖍 **+** 🖍 🖍 🖍 **=**
_____

Name_____ Date_____

Addition

Directions: Add the pictures. Write the answer on the line.

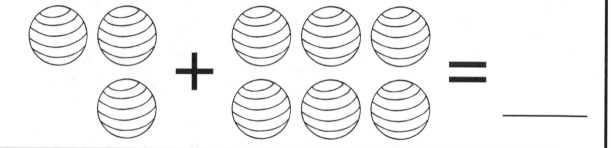

= 10

+ = _____

+ = _____

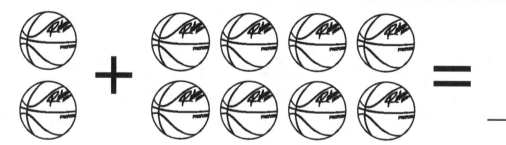

+ = _____

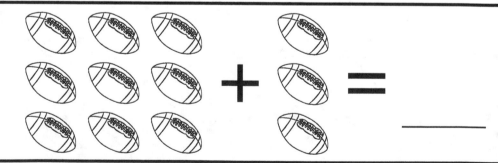

+ = _____

 Addition

Directions: Add the pictures, and write the answer on the line.

4 + 1 = _____

2 + 3 = _____

1 + 0 = _____

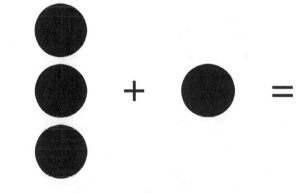

3 + 1 = _____

1 + 1 = _____

0 + 3 = _____

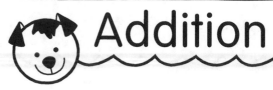

Addition

Directions: Add the numbers, and write the answer.

2
+ 1
3

4
+ 0

3
+ 2

1
+ 1

1
+ 3

0
+ 5

2
+ 2

4
+ 1

 # Addition

Directions: Circle the number sentence that matches the picture.

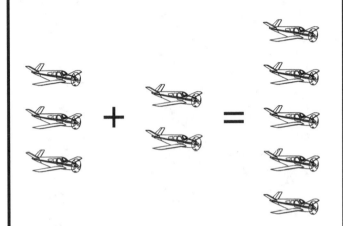

a. 3 + 2 = 5
b. 3 + 1 = 4

a. 1 + 3 = 4
b. 1 + 4 = 5

a. 3 + 3 = 6
b. 2 + 2 = 4

a. 1 + 2 = 3
b. 2 + 2 = 4

 # Addition

Directions: Write the number sentence that matches the pictures.

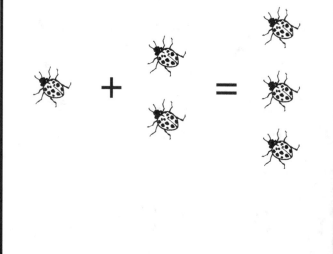

_____ + _____ = _____   _____ + _____ = _____

_____ + _____ = _____   _____ + _____ = _____

 # Addition

Directions: Add the pictures, and write the answer on the line.

$4 + 2 = \underline{6}$

$5 + 3 = \underline{}$

$4 + 4 = \underline{}$

$3 + 3 = \underline{}$

Addition

Directions: Add the numbers, and write the answer.

1 ✿	6 ●●●●●●
+ 5 ✿✿✿✿✿	+ 2 ●●
͙6͙	

| 8 ▲▲▲▲▲▲▲▲ | 5 ✿✿✿✿✿ |
| + 0 | + 2 ✿✿ |

 Addition

Directions: Circle the number sentence that matches the pictures.

a. 5 + 2 = 7
b. 5 + 3 = 8

a. 2 + 4 = 6
b. 2 + 6 = 8

a. 4 + 3 = 7
b. 3 + 3 = 6

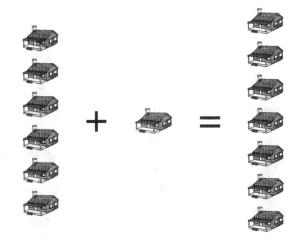

a. 5 + 1 = 6
b. 6 + 1 = 7

Addition

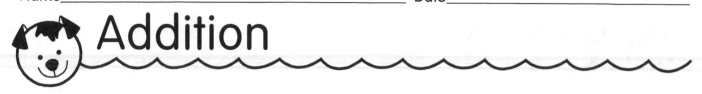

Directions: Write the number sentence that matches the pictures.

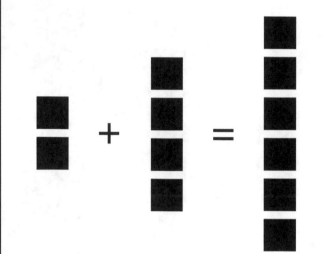

$$2 + 4 = 6$$

_____ + _____ = _____

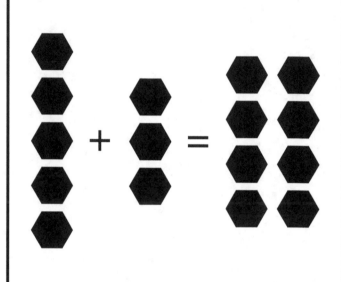

_____ + _____ = _____

_____ + _____ = _____

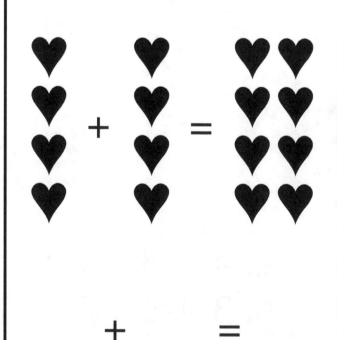

_____ + _____ = _____

Name_____   Date_____

 Addition

Directions: Draw one more picture, and fill in the missing numbers in the number sentence.

3 + 1 = 4

____ + 1 = ____

____ + 1 = ____

____ + 1 = ____

____ + 1 = ____

____ + 1 = ____

Name_____   Date_____

Addition

Directions: Add the pictures, and write the answer on the line.

$2 + 8 =$ __10__

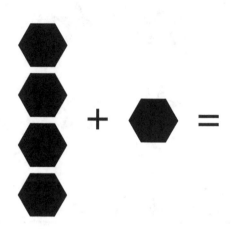

$4 + 1 =$ _____

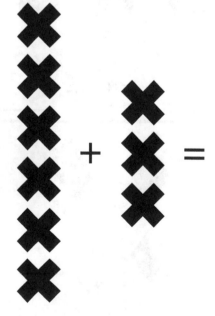

$6 + 3 =$ _____

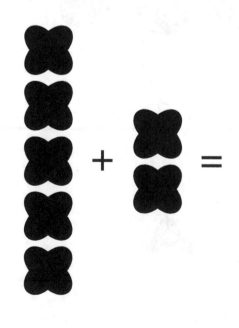

$5 + 2 =$ _____

Addition

Directions: Add the numbers, and write the answer.

5
+ 5
10

4
+ 5

7
+ 2

6
+ 4

Addition

Directions: Circle the number sentence that matches the picture.

a. 7 + 2 = 9
b. 8 + 2 = 10

a. 3 + 6 = 9
b. 5 + 5 = 10

a. 4 + 6 = 10
b. 5 + 4 = 9

a. 3 + 6 = 9
b. 3 + 5 = 8

Addition

Directions: Write the number sentence that matches the pictures.

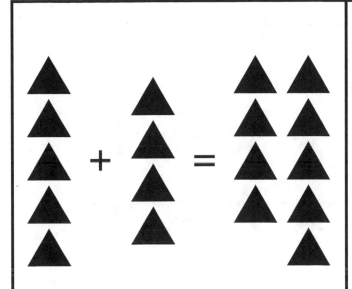

5 + 4 = 9

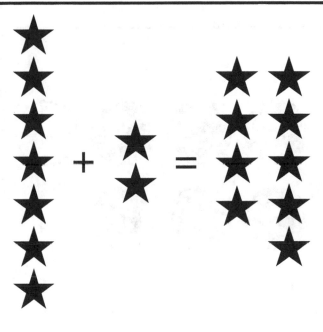

___ + ___ = ___

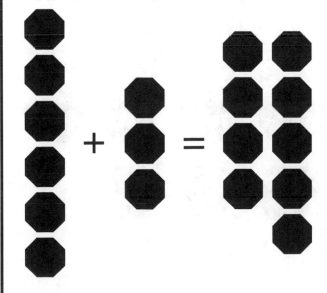

___ + ___ = ___

___ + ___ = ___

Name_____ Date_____

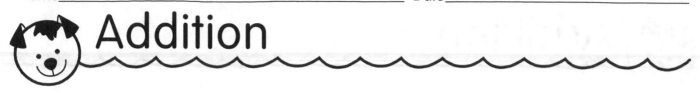

Addition

Directions: Draw one more picture, and fill in the missing numbers in the number sentence.

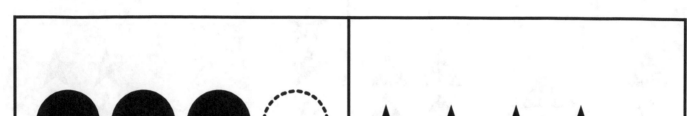

___6___ + 1 = ___7___   _____ + 1 = _____

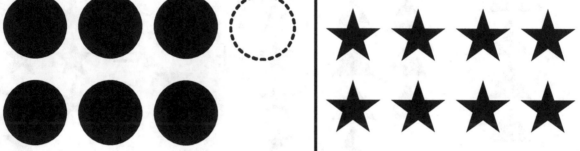

_____ + 1 = _____   _____ + 1 = _____

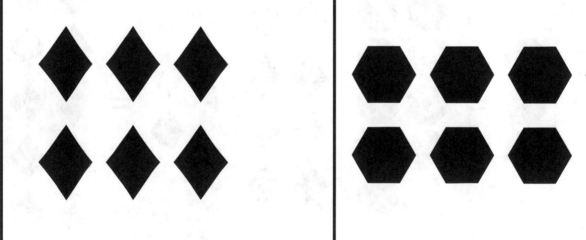

Addition

Directions: Add the pictures, and write the answer on the line.

4 + 8 = 12

6 + 5 = ____

7 + 4 = ____

6 + 6 = ____

Addition

Directions: Add the numbers, and write the answer.

2 ⬡ ⬡
+ 9 ⬡ ⬡ ⬡ ⬡ ⬡ ⬡ ⬡ ⬡ ⬡
¦ ¦ ¦

8 ✗ ✗ ✗ ✗ ✗ ✗ ✗ ✗
+ 3 ✗ ✗ ✗

9 ▲ ▲ ▲ ▲ ▲ ▲ ▲ ▲ ▲
+ 3 ▲ ▲ ▲

7 ◆ ◆ ◆ ◆ ◆ ◆ ◆
+ 5 ◆ ◆ ◆ ◆ ◆

Addition

Directions: Circle the number sentence that matches the pictures.

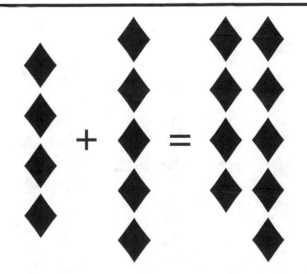

a. 6 + 6 = 12

b. 5 + 5 = 10

a. 9 + 2 = 11

b. 7 + 5 = 12

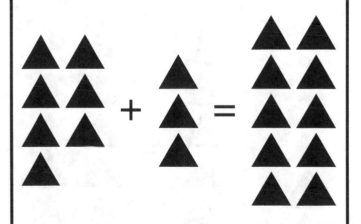

a. 4 + 5 = 9

b. 8 + 4 = 12

a. 6 + 5 = 11

b. 7 + 3 = 10

Addition

Directions: Write the number sentence that matches the pictures.

$$3 + 8 = 11$$

____ + ____ = ____

____ + ____ = ____

____ + ____ = ____

____ + ____ = ____

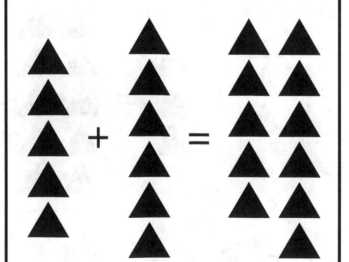

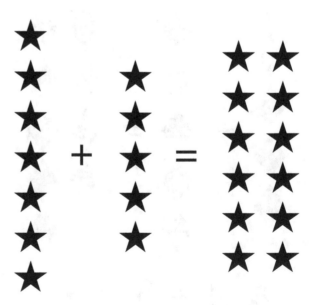

Name_____ Date_____

Addition Unit Test

Directions: Add the pictures, and fill in the circle next to the answer.

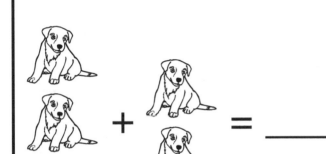

○ 4   ○ 5   ○ 6

+ = ____

○ 5   ○ 3   ○ 4

 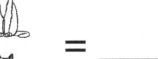

○ 5   ○ 7   ○ 4

○ 2   ○ 3   ○ 5

Addition and Subtraction   **25**

Addition Unit Test

Directions: Fill in the circle next to the number sentence that matches the pictures.

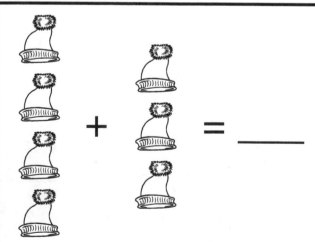

○ 1 + 3 = 4
○ 3 + 2 = 5
○ 3 + 3 = 6

○ 2 + 1 = 3
○ 3 + 3 = 6
○ 4 + 1 = 5

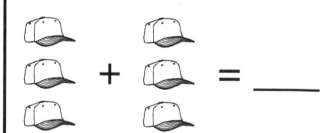

○ 4 + 3 = 7
○ 3 + 2 = 5
○ 2 + 4 = 6

○ 3 + 3 = 6
○ 1 + 4 = 5
○ 1 + 3 = 4

Name_____   Date_____

Addition Unit Test

Directions: Add the pictures, and fill in the circle next to the answer.

○ 9   ○ 8   ○ 7

○ 8   ○ 9   ○ 6

 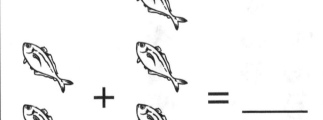

○ 5   ○ 4   ○ 6

○ 7   ○ 9   ○ 10

Addition Unit Test

Directions: Fill in the circle next to the number sentence that matches the pictures.

▮ + ▮ = _____

○ 6 + 6 = 12

○ 7 + 3 = 10

○ 9 + 2 = 11

● + ● = _____

○ 5 + 5 = 10

○ 8 + 4 = 12

○ 6 + 4 = 10

▲ + ▲ = _____

○ 6 + 5 = 11

○ 8 + 2 = 10

○ 9 + 3 = 12

⬡ + ⬡ = _____

○ 3 + 8 = 11

○ 7 + 4 = 11

○ 5 + 7 = 12

Subtraction

Directions: The pizza slices that were eaten are crossed out. Count the pizza slices that are not crossed out to find out how many are left.

Eat 1, __2__ left

Eat 1, ____ left

Eat 1, ____ left

Eat 1, ____ left

Name_____ Date_____

 Subtraction

Directions: The cookies that were eaten are crossed out. Count the cookies that are not crossed out to find out how many are left.

Eat 3, left

Eat 1, ___ left

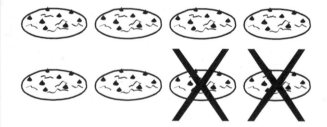

Eat 2, ___ left

Eat 4, ___ left

Eat 0, ___ left

Eat 1, ___ left

Name_____ Date_____

 # Subtraction

Directions: The fruits that were eaten are crossed out. Count the fruits that are not crossed out to find out how many are left.

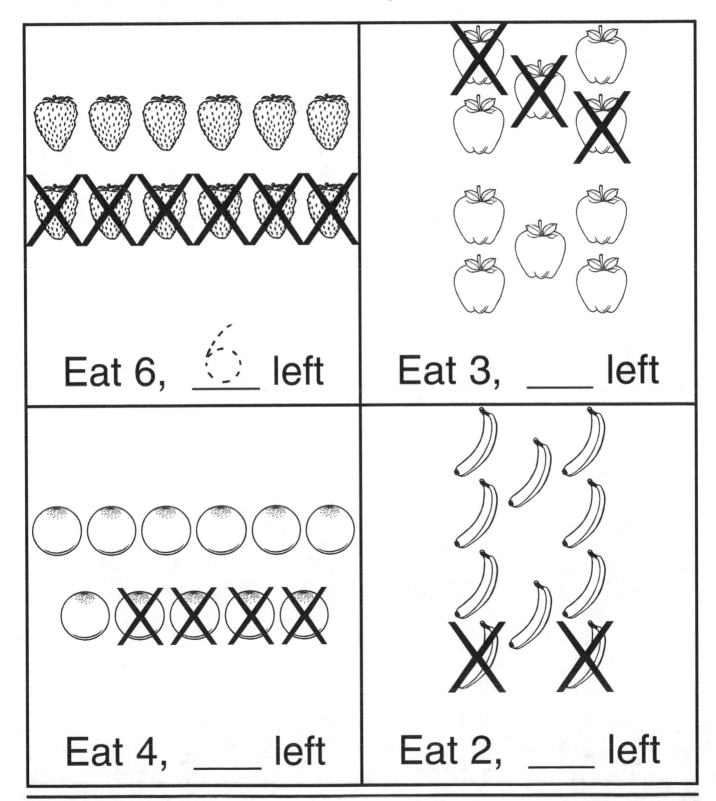

Eat 6, _6_ left

Eat 3, ___ left

Eat 4, ___ left

Eat 2, ___ left

Name_____   Date_____

Subtraction

Directions: Cross out one picture to subtract one, and write the answer.

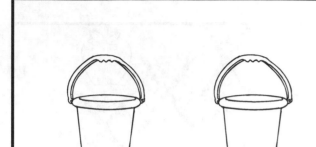

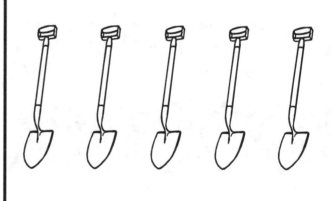

4 – 1 = __3__

5 – 1 = _____

2 – 1 = _____

3 – 1 = _____

Name_____ Date_____

Subtraction

Directions: Cross out the number of pictures to match the equation, and write the answer.

$$\begin{array}{r} 2 \\ -\ 1 \\ \hline \end{array}$$

$$\begin{array}{r} 4 \\ -\ 0 \\ \hline \end{array}$$

$$\begin{array}{r} 3 \\ -\ 2 \\ \hline \end{array}$$

$$\begin{array}{r} 1 \\ -\ 1 \\ \hline \end{array}$$

$$\begin{array}{r} 3 \\ -\ 1 \\ \hline \end{array}$$

$$\begin{array}{r} 5 \\ -\ 2 \\ \hline \end{array}$$

Subtraction

Directions: Circle the number sentence that matches the picture.

a. 5 – 3 = 2
b. 5 – 2 = 3

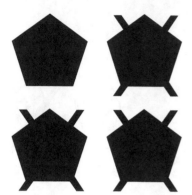

a. 4 – 3 = 1
b. 4 – 1 = 3

a. 5 – 1 = 4
b. 5 – 4 = 1

a. 4 – 4 = 0
b. 4 – 0 = 4

Name_____ Date_____

Subtraction

Directions: Write the number sentence that matches the pictures.

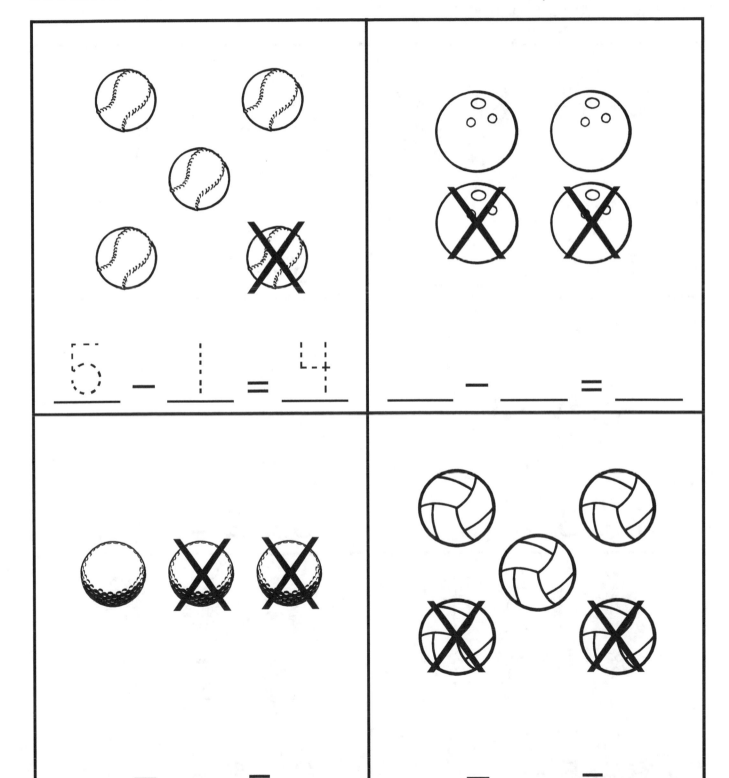

5 – 1 = 4

___ – ___ = ___

___ – ___ = ___

___ – ___ = ___

Name_____   Date_____

Subtraction

Directions: Cross out the number of pictures to match the number sentence. Write the answer.

4 – 2 = 2

5 – 1 = _____

7 – 3 = _____

3 – 2 = _____

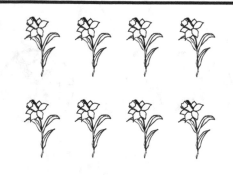

8 – 5 = _____

6 – 3 = _____

Subtraction

Directions: Cross out the number of pictures to match the equation, and write the answer.

$$\begin{array}{r} 8 \\ -\ 4 \\ \hline \end{array}$$

$$\begin{array}{r} 8 \\ -\ 6 \\ \hline \end{array}$$

$$\begin{array}{r} 7 \\ -\ 5 \\ \hline \end{array}$$

$$\begin{array}{r} 6 \\ -\ 5 \\ \hline \end{array}$$

Subtraction

Directions: Circle the number sentence that matches the picture.

a. 7 − 5 = 2
b. 7 − 2 = 5

a. 8 − 5 = 3
b. 8 − 6 = 2

a. 6 − 5 = 1
b. 6 − 1 = 5

a. 7 − 3 = 4
b. 7 − 4 = 3

Name_____ Date_____

Subtraction

Directions: Write the number sentence that matches the pictures.

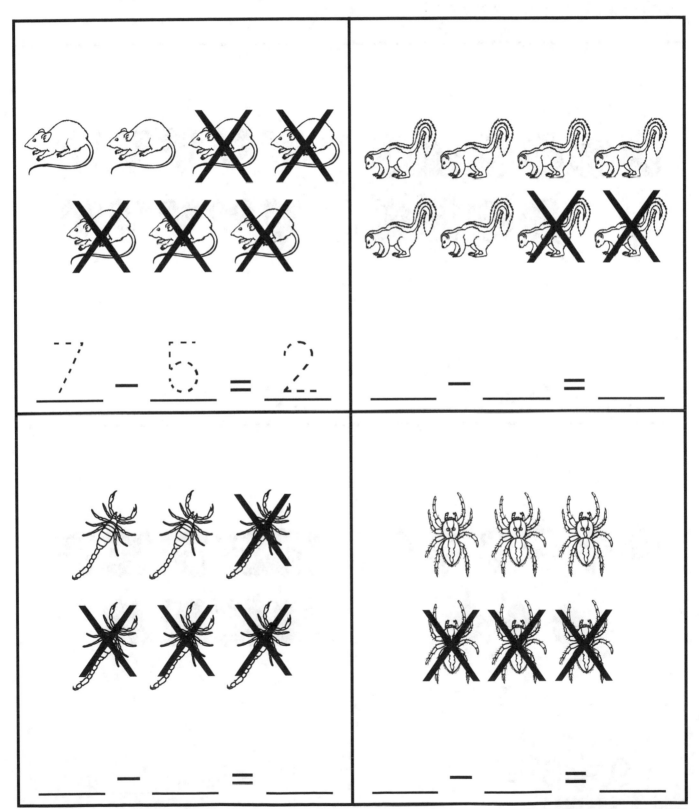

7 - 5 = 2

___ - ___ = ___

___ - ___ = ___

___ - ___ = ___

Subtraction

Directions: Cross out the number of pictures to match the number sentence. Write the answer.

10 − 6 = __4__

10 − 5 = _____

9 − 3 = _____

9 − 4 = _____

 # Subtraction

Directions: Cross out the number of pictures to match the equation, and write the answer.

10
− 5
_____
5

9
− 3
_____

10
− 2
_____

9
− 5
_____

Subtraction

Directions: Circle the number sentence that matches the picture.

a. $10 - 6 = 4$
b. $10 - 4 = 6$

a. $9 - 3 = 6$
b. $9 - 6 = 3$

a. $10 - 1 = 9$
b. $10 - 9 = 1$

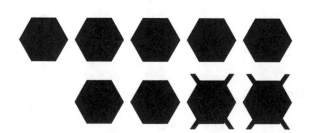

a. $9 - 5 = 4$
b. $9 - 2 = 7$

Substraction

Directions: Write the number sentence that matches the pictures.

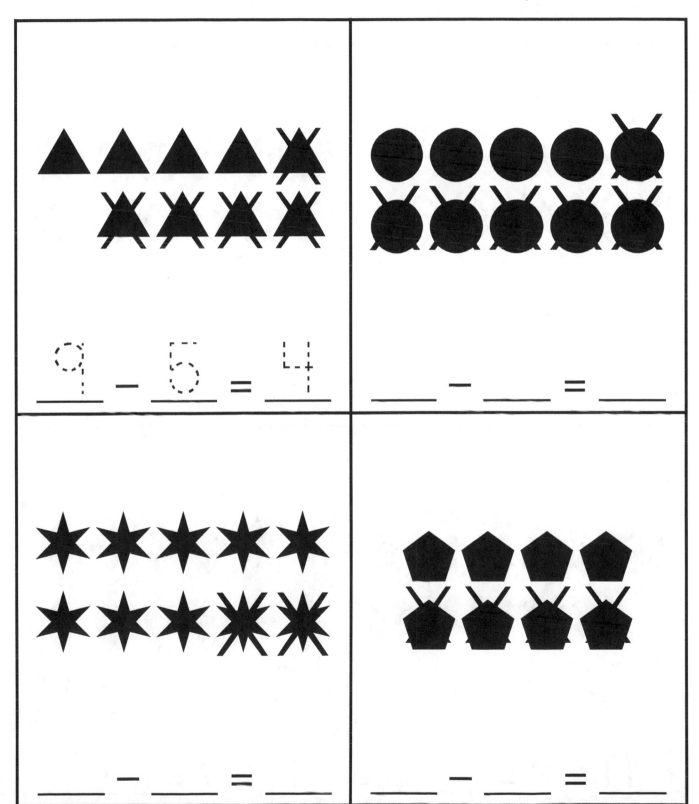

9 − 5 = 4

___ − ___ = ___

___ − ___ = ___

___ − ___ = ___

Subtraction

Directions: Cross out the number of pictures to match the number sentence. Write the answer.

★ ★ ★ ★ ★ ★
✳ ✳ ✳ ✳ ✳

12 – 6 = _6_

❀ ❀ ❀ ❀ ❀ ❀
❀ ❀ ❀ ❀ ❀ ❀

12 – 8 = _____

✕ ✕ ✕ ✕ ✕ ✕
✕ ✕ ✕ ✕ ✕

11 – 6 = _____

◆ ◆ ◆ ◆ ◆
◆ ◆ ◆ ◆ ◆ ◆

11 – 7 = _____

Subtraction

Directions: Cross out the number of pictures to match the equation, and write the answer.

12
− 4
___
8

☆☆☆☆☆☆☆☆

12
− 9
___

11
− 7
___

STOP STOP STOP STOP STOP STOP STOP
STOP STOP STOP STOP

11
− 8
___

✚✚✚✚✚✚✚✚
✚✚✚

Subtraction

Directions: Circle the number sentence that matches the picture.

a. 10 – 6 = 4

b. 11 – 4 = 7

a. 12 – 7 = 5

b. 12 – 3 = 9

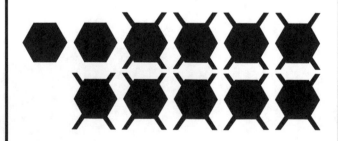

a. 11 – 9 = 2

b. 10 – 4 = 6

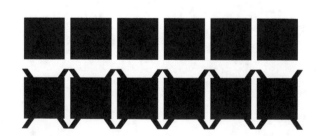

a. 12 – 6 = 6

b. 12 – 9 = 3

Subtraction

Directions: Write the number sentence that matches the pictures.

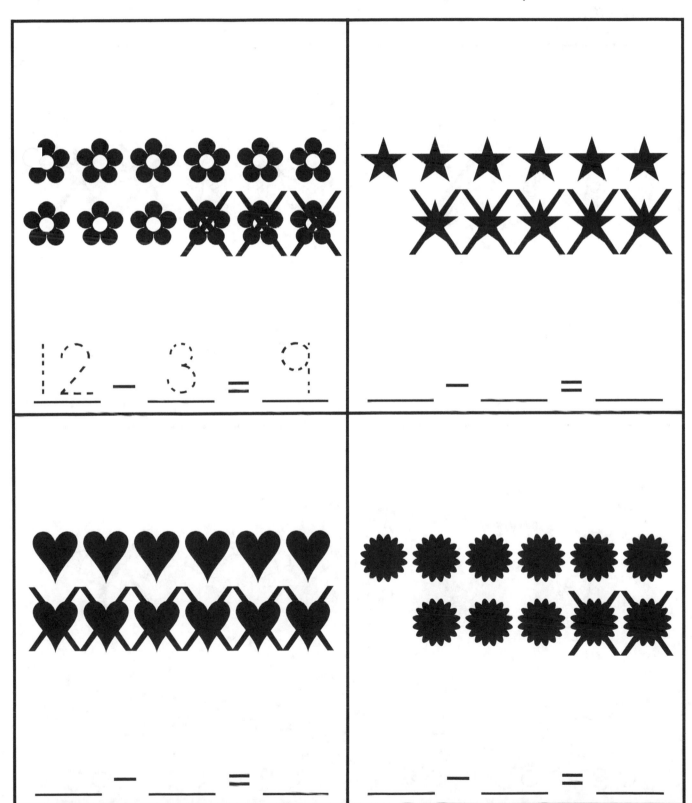

12 – 3 = 9

___ – ___ = ___

___ – ___ = ___

___ – ___ = ___

Subtraction Unit Test

Directions: Subtract the crossed out pictures, and fill in the circle next to the answer.

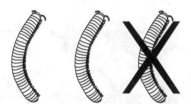

3 – 1 = _____

○ 2   ○ 3   ○ 1

4 – 2 = _____

○ 3   ○ 2   ○ 1

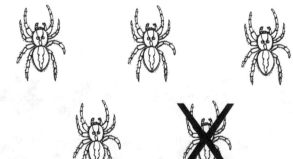

5 – 1 = _____

○ 5   ○ 3   ○ 4

2 – 1 = _____

○ 2   ○ 1   ○ 3

Subtraction Unit Test

Directions: Fill in the circle next to the number sentence that matches the picture.

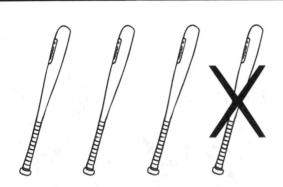

○ $3 - 1 = 2$

○ $5 - 2 = 3$

○ $4 - 1 = 3$

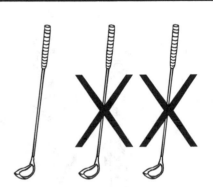

○ $2 - 1 = 1$

○ $3 - 2 = 1$

○ $4 - 2 = 2$

○ $5 - 2 = 3$

○ $4 - 1 = 3$

○ $5 - 4 = 1$

○ $4 - 2 = 2$

○ $5 - 4 = 1$

○ $6 - 4 = 2$

Name_____ Date_____

Subtraction Unit Test

Directions: Subtract the crossed out pictures and fill in the circle next to the answer.

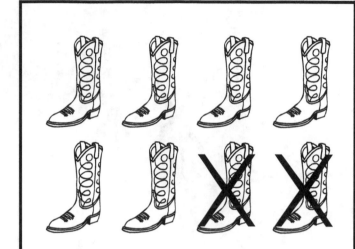

$8 - 2 =$ _____

○ 6   ○ 4   ○ 8

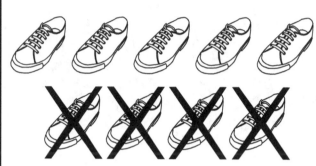

$9 - 4 =$ _____

○ 6   ○ 8   ○ 5

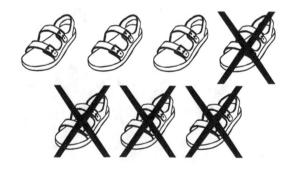

$7 - 4 =$ _____

○ 5   ○ 3   ○ 4

$6 - 1 =$ _____

○ 7   ○ 5   ○ 3

Subtraction Unit Test

Directions: Fill in the circle next to the number sentence that matches the picture.

○ $10 - 6 = 4$

○ $9 - 2 = 7$

○ $10 - 4 = 6$

○ $9 - 5 = 4$

○ $9 - 2 = 7$

○ $9 - 6 = 3$

○ $11 - 2 = 9$

○ $10 - 5 = 5$

○ $11 - 4 = 7$

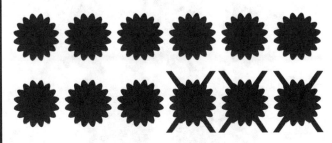

○ $12 - 6 = 6$

○ $12 - 8 = 4$

○ $12 - 3 = 9$

Name_____ Date_____

Addition/Subtraction Test

Directions: Fill in the circle next to the answer for each number sentence.

$$4 - 2 = \underline{\hspace{2cm}}$$

○ 2   ○ 3   ○ 4

 + =

$$3 + 1 = \underline{\hspace{2cm}}$$

○ 4   ○ 2   ○ 5

$$5 - 4 = \underline{\hspace{2cm}}$$

○ 3   ○ 1   ○ 4

+ =

$$1 + 1 = \underline{\hspace{2cm}}$$

○ 2   ○ 3   ○ 4

Addition/Subtraction Test

Directions: Fill in the circle next to the answer for each number sentence.

5 + 4 = _____

○ 7　　○ 9　　○ 8

9 – 6 = _____

○ 4　　○ 3　　○ 5

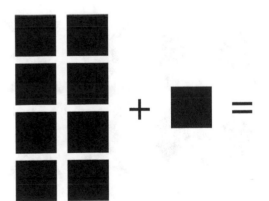

8 + 1 = _____

○ 9　　○ 7　　○ 6

7 – 5 = _____

○ 1　　○ 2　　○ 4

Addition/Subtraction Test

Directions: Fill in the circle next to the answer for each number sentence.

4 + 3 = _____

○ 8   ○ 7   ○ 6

7 − 2 = _____

○ 5   ○ 3   ○ 4

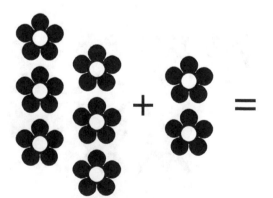

6 + 2 = _____

○ 7   ○ 8   ○ 9

8 − 4 = _____

○ 6   ○ 5   ○ 4

Answer Key pages 1–9

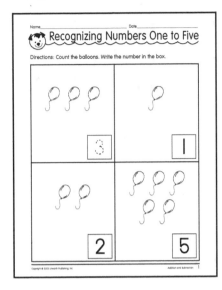

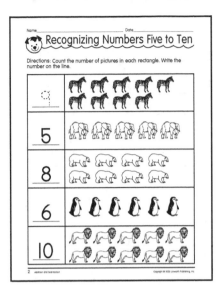

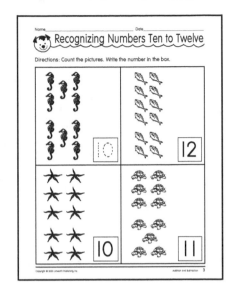

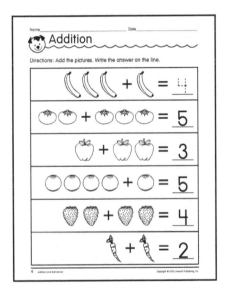

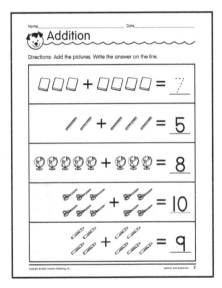

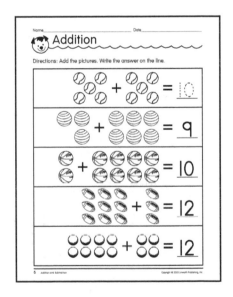

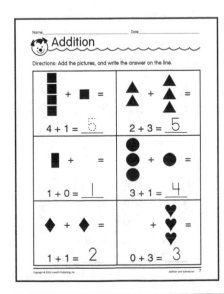

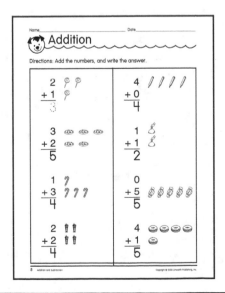

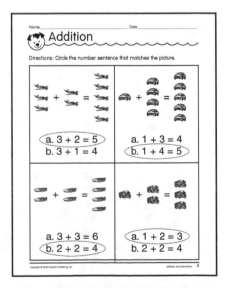

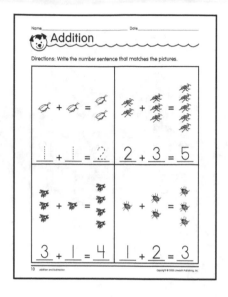

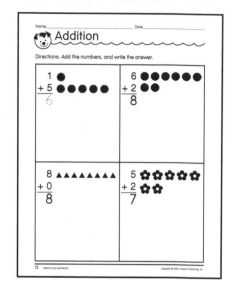

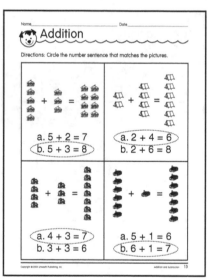

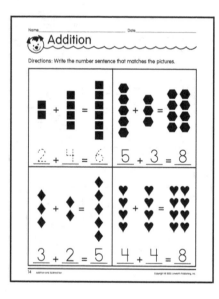

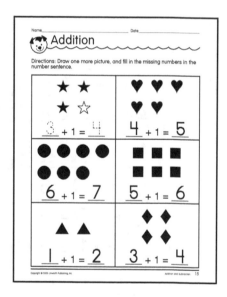

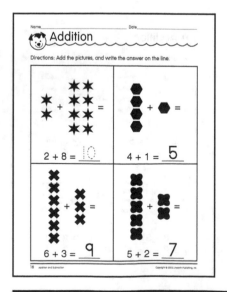

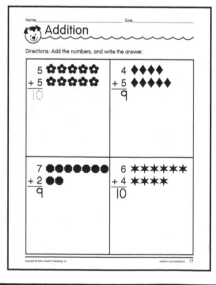

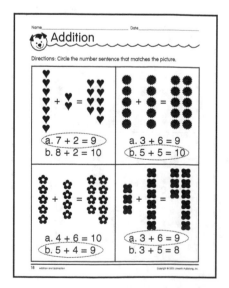

Answer Key pages 19–27

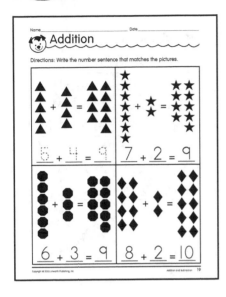

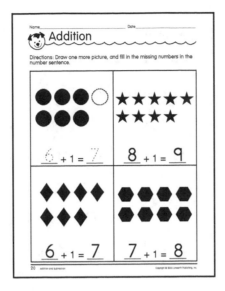

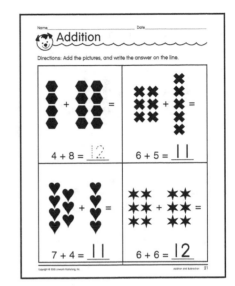

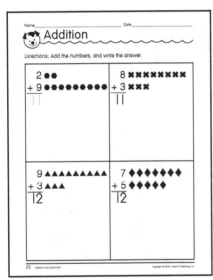

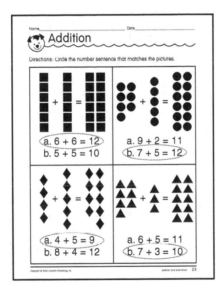

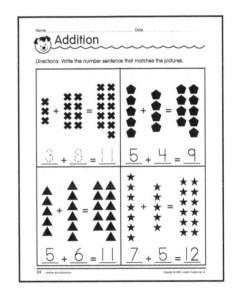

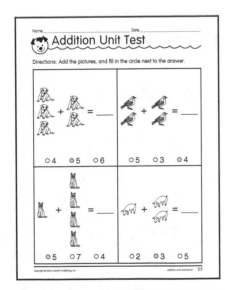

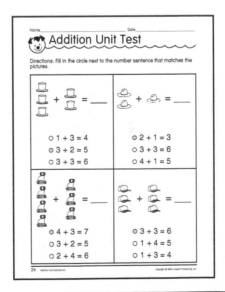

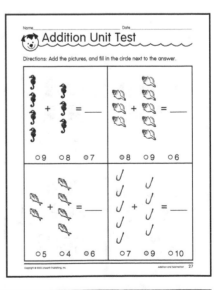

Answer Key pages 28–36

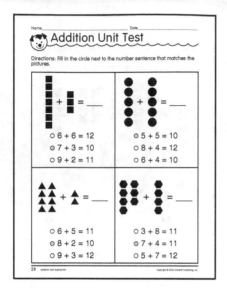

Addition Unit Test

Directions: Fill in the circle next to the number sentence that matches the pictures.

○ 6 + 6 = 12
○ 7 + 3 = 10
○ 9 + 2 = 11

○ 5 + 5 = 10
○ 8 + 4 = 12
○ 6 + 4 = 10

○ 6 + 5 = 11
○ 8 + 2 = 10
○ 9 + 3 = 12

○ 3 + 8 = 11
○ 7 + 4 = 11
○ 5 + 7 = 12

28 Addition and Subtraction

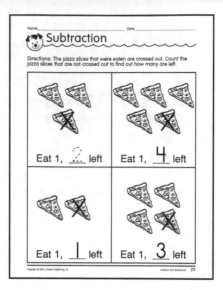

Subtraction

Directions: The pizza slices that were eaten are crossed out. Count the pizza slices that are not crossed out to find out how many are left.

Eat 1, _2_ left   Eat 1, _4_ left

Eat 1, _1_ left   Eat 1, _3_ left

29 Addition and Subtraction

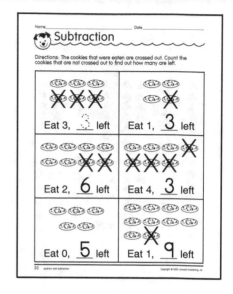

Subtraction

Directions: The cookies that were eaten are crossed out. Count the cookies that are not crossed out to find out how many are left.

Eat 3, _3_ left   Eat 1, _3_ left

Eat 2, _6_ left   Eat 4, _3_ left

Eat 0, _5_ left   Eat 1, _9_ left

30 Addition and Subtraction

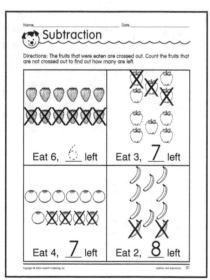

Subtraction

Directions: The fruits that were eaten are crossed out. Count the fruits that are not crossed out to find out how many are left.

Eat 6, _6_ left   Eat 3, _7_ left

Eat 4, _7_ left   Eat 2, _8_ left

31 Addition and Subtraction

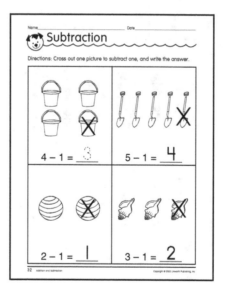

Subtraction

Directions: Cross out one picture to subtract one, and write the answer.

4 − 1 = _3_   5 − 1 = _4_

2 − 1 = _1_   3 − 1 = _2_

32 Addition and Subtraction

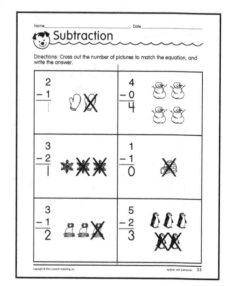

Subtraction

Directions: Cross out the number of pictures to match the equation, and write the answer.

2
− 1
___
_1_

4
− 0
___
_4_

3
− 2
___
_1_

1
− 1
___
_0_

3
− 1
___
_2_

5
− 2
___
_3_

33 Addition and Subtraction

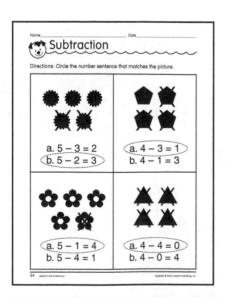

Subtraction

Directions: Circle the number sentence that matches the picture.

a. 5 − 3 = 2
(b. 5 − 2 = 3)

(a. 4 − 3 = 1)
b. 4 − 1 = 3

(a. 5 − 1 = 4)
b. 5 − 4 = 1

(a. 4 − 4 = 0)
b. 4 − 0 = 4

34 Addition and Subtraction

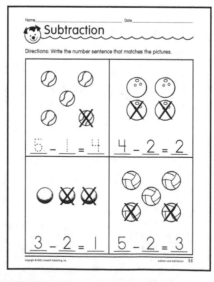

Subtraction

Directions: Write the number sentence that matches the pictures.

_5_ − _1_ = _4_   _4_ − _2_ = 2

_3_ − _2_ = 1   _5_ − _2_ = _3_

35 Addition and Subtraction

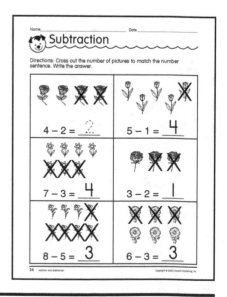

Subtraction

Directions: Cross out the number of pictures to match the number sentence. Write the answer.

4 − 2 = _2_   5 − 1 = _4_

7 − 3 = _4_   3 − 2 = _1_

8 − 5 = _3_   6 − 3 = _3_

36 Addition and Subtraction

58   Addition and Subtraction

Answer Key pages 37–45

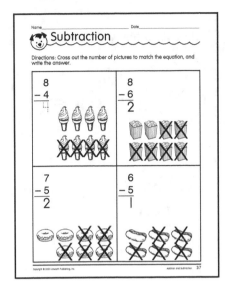

Name_____ Date_____

Subtraction

Directions: Cross out the number of pictures to match the equation, and write the answer.

$\begin{array}{r} 8 \\ -4 \\ \hline 4 \end{array}$

$\begin{array}{r} 8 \\ -6 \\ \hline 2 \end{array}$

$\begin{array}{r} 7 \\ -5 \\ \hline 2 \end{array}$

$\begin{array}{r} 6 \\ -5 \\ \hline 1 \end{array}$

37

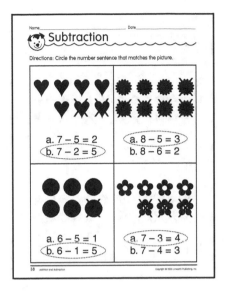

Subtraction

Directions: Circle the number sentence that matches the picture.

a. $7 - 5 = 2$
b. $7 - 2 = 5$

a. $8 - 5 = 3$
b. $8 - 6 = 2$

a. $6 - 5 = 1$
b. $6 - 1 = 5$

a. $7 - 3 = 4$
b. $7 - 4 = 3$

38

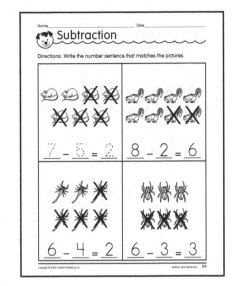

Subtraction

Directions: Write the number sentence that matches the pictures.

$7 - 5 = 2$

$8 - 2 = 6$

$6 - 4 = 2$

$6 - 3 = 3$

39

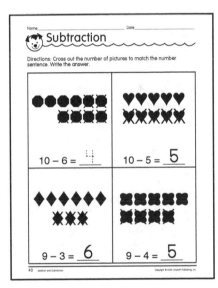

Subtraction

Directions: Cross out the number of pictures to match the number sentence. Write the answer.

$10 - 6 = 4$

$10 - 5 = 5$

$9 - 3 = 6$

$9 - 4 = 5$

40

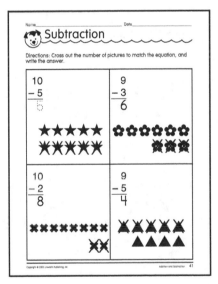

Subtraction

Directions: Cross out the number of pictures to match the equation, and write the answer.

$\begin{array}{r} 10 \\ -5 \\ \hline 5 \end{array}$

$\begin{array}{r} 9 \\ -3 \\ \hline 6 \end{array}$

$\begin{array}{r} 10 \\ -2 \\ \hline 8 \end{array}$

$\begin{array}{r} 9 \\ -5 \\ \hline 4 \end{array}$

41

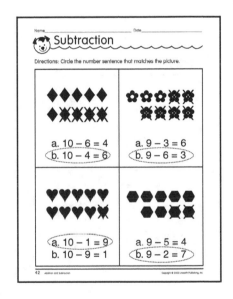

Subtraction

Directions: Circle the number sentence that matches the picture.

a. $10 - 6 = 4$
b. $10 - 4 = 6$

a. $9 - 3 = 6$
b. $9 - 6 = 3$

a. $10 - 1 = 9$
b. $10 - 9 = 1$

a. $9 - 5 = 4$
b. $9 - 2 = 7$

42

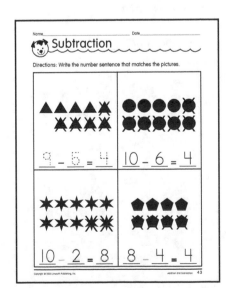

Subtraction

Directions: Write the number sentence that matches the pictures.

$9 - 5 = 4$

$10 - 6 = 4$

$10 - 2 = 8$

$8 - 4 = 4$

43

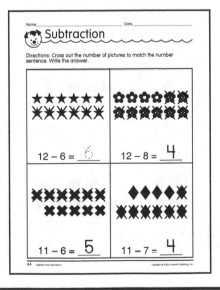

Subtraction

Directions: Cross out the number of pictures to match the number sentence. Write the answer.

$12 - 6 = 6$

$12 - 8 = 4$

$11 - 6 = 5$

$11 - 7 = 4$

44

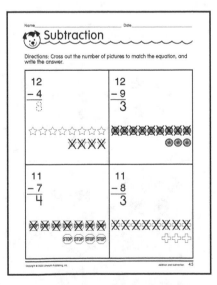

Subtraction

Directions: Cross out the number of pictures to match the equation, and write the answer.

$\begin{array}{r} 12 \\ -4 \\ \hline 8 \end{array}$

$\begin{array}{r} 12 \\ -9 \\ \hline 3 \end{array}$

$\begin{array}{r} 11 \\ -7 \\ \hline 4 \end{array}$

$\begin{array}{r} 11 \\ -8 \\ \hline 3 \end{array}$

45

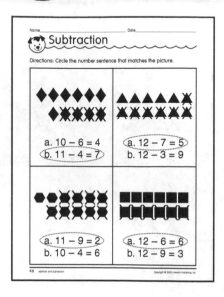
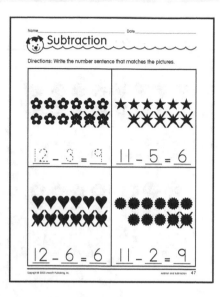
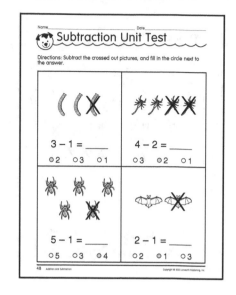

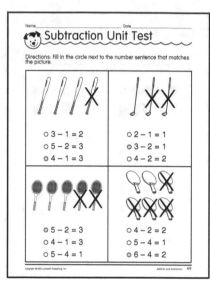
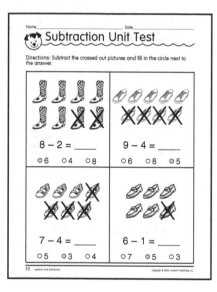
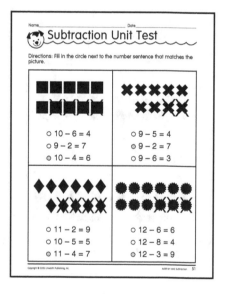

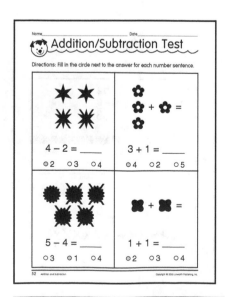
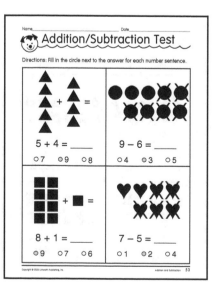
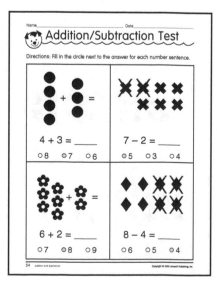

Answer Key pages 46–54

60   Addition and Subtraction

Copyright © 2003 Linworth Publishing, Inc.

Printed in the USA
CPSIA information can be obtained
at www.ICGtesting.com
LVHW080723170724
785510LV00007B/285